GIRLS
Who Looked
Under
Rocks

The Lives of Six Pioneering Naturalists

by Jeannine Atkins
Illustrated by Paula Conner

Dawn Publications

To Alice and Donald Laird —JA

This, my first published work as an illustrator, is lovingly dedicated to my children, Amanda, Greg, Stephen and Michael, adventurers all, and to my own rock-hound—my dear, patient husband, Scott. —PC

Library of Congress Cataloging-in-Publication Data

Atkins, Jeannine, 1953-
 Girls who looked under rocks : the lives of six pioneering naturalists / by Jeannine Atkins ; illustrated by Paula Conner.
     p. cm.
Includes bibliographical references.
 ISBN 1-58469-011-9 (pbk.)
 1. Naturalists—Biography—Juvenile literature. 2. Women naturalists—Biography—Juvenile literature. [1. Naturalists. 2. Women—Biography.] I. Conner, Paula, ill. II. Title.
 QH26 .A75 2000
 508'.092'2—dc21
                                                    00-008829

DAWN Publications
P.O. Box 2010
Nevada City, CA 95959
800-545-7475
Email: nature@DawnPub.com
Website: www.DawnPub.com

Printed in the United States of America

10 9 8 7 6 5 4 3 2
First Edition

Design and computer production by Andrea Miles

Contents

Introduction

The six women portrayed in this book all grew up to become award-winning scientists and writers, as comfortable with a pen as with a magnifying glass. They all started out as girls who didn't run from spiders or snakes, but crouched down to take a closer look.

When choosing whom to profile in this book, I was drawn to women who found beauty in unlikely places. I couldn't resist writing about a nineteenth century lady who snatched a wasp at a tea party, pulled her collecting case from the folds of her long dress, and quietly tucked away her prize. In the twentieth century it became more common to find women hunched over microscopes or hiking alone in forests, but a scientific interest in caterpillars, chickens, and chimpanzees was still considered unconventional. These naturalists were too busy watching animals to mind who was or wasn't watching them. They never stopped climbing trees when they grew up.

Maria Sibylla Merian sailed from Holland to South America in 1699 to learn about beetles, butterflies, and some quite spectacular spiders. In a time when naturalists made guides with plants and animals treated separately, Maria painted plants and insects in the same picture. Her work led to a greater understanding of how all kinds of lives depend upon each other.

Anna Comstock was one of the first women to earn a degree in entomology, the study of insects. By writing books and teaching teachers, Anna helped start a movement to include nature study in schools.

Frances Hamerstrom took twelve years of ballroom dancing lessons and wore gowns gracefully enough to become a fashion model, but she gave this up to spend more than fifty years wearing flannel shirts and hiking boots in the mid-western prairies. Frances was one of the first field biologists, those amazing people who spend hours of their days, and years of their lives, watching animals. What they observe helps us learn not only more about the particular animal studied, but more about life in general.

Miriam Rothschild was raised in a mansion, but when she grew up she let the trimmed lawns and elegant gardens grow wild with the weeds that butterflies preferred. As a highly respected entomologist, Miriam's concern for the smallest fleas, moths, and butterflies led to a concern for the entire world.

Rachel Carson had a mother who didn't blink, at least much, at finding six-legged creatures in her daughter's bureaus. Rachel overcame her shyness to write and speak about the dangers of pesticides. Her best-selling book, *Silent Spring,* shows how changing one small part of nature can upset the balance of the whole.

Jane Goodall watched bugs in her backyard as a girl. Later she used her curiosity and patience studying chimpanzees in Africa. Her observation that the chimpanzees used tools showed that the differences between human animals and other animals may not be as great as many thought. Jane is now committed to helping people around the world see other lives with compassion.

Often these naturalists were the only women among men in their fields. As outsiders, they sometimes questioned things others took for granted, such as a scientist's need for detachment. All might have agreed with Jane Goodall that her feeling for animals was a strength, rather than a weakness. These women were passionate scientists. They often worked alone, but they also taught enthusiastically, wrote energetically, and found ways to pass on their vision of how all lives are beautifully connected. Their stories remind us to look and to look harder and then to look again. Under rotten logs or in puddles, there are amazing things to see.

I.

Maria Sibylla Merian

Following Butterflies
(1647-1717)

AINTBRUSHES SWISHED and scraped across canvas. The parlor smelled faintly of wood, as blocks were carved for prints. Some visitors were struck by the girl who stood painting between her brothers. In the 1600's, fathers in Germany often taught a trade to their sons, but daughters were expected to learn only cooking and sewing from their mothers.

"It's a waste of time to teach painting to a girl," people said. "There's never been a great woman artist." Maria's stepfather shrugged rather than argue; perhaps that was because no girl had ever been given lessons, he thought. Besides, he didn't expect to make enough money to give Maria much of a dowry when she got married. It seemed foolish not to give her what he had. He simply advised Maria that her flower paintings might be more popular if she didn't put bees and beetles on the leaves.

But insects were Maria's favorite part of a picture. She rarely left the house without a net. She searched through neighbors' gardens and around the moat of her village for butterflies and spiders. She brought home caterpillars that were raised for their silk, fed them mulberry leaves, and watched them spin cocoons.

By the time she was thirteen, Maria had decided to specialize in painting insects. Moved by God's attention to such small beings, she copied the fuzzy texture of an antenna and the tiny holes left by caterpillars nibbling on leaves. Her only tool was a magnifying glass, but her details were so fine that one could almost hear the hum and buzz.

Maria rarely left the house without a net.

Maria knew she had much to be thankful for, but she still sometim

lt as a caterpillar might while waiting to burst from its cocoon.

As Maria grew older, other German artists admired the beauty in her work and scientists praised its accuracy. She painted moths and butterflies larger than life so that people could plainly see the extraordinary patterns on their wings. Her work brought good prices, but as she watched butterflies perch only briefly before fluttering off to blend into the blue sky, she yearned to see the places where they landed.

Maria hoped her restlessness would end after she married, then gave birth to two girls. Her paints and caterpillar breeding boxes shared space with the pots in the kitchen. The baby's laughter mixed with the sounds of paintbrush strokes and wasps buzzing around the nest they had built beside the hearth. Maria knew she had much to be thankful for, but she still sometimes felt as a caterpillar might while waiting to burst from its cocoon.

When she heard of a religious community where people shared everything, she hoped she could humbly put away her longing to see more. She thought she should stay in one place and learn to be content with a simpler life. "I won't give away our fine things!" Maria's husband said. But Maria insisted. "Why should we have fancy clothes and furniture when others go hungry? I have to go there." She realized that her husband would leave her if she went. She worried about her children growing up without a father, but she truly believed that she had found a kinder way to live.

At the Christian community, everyone took part in the house and farm work. Maria taught her daughters and other children to sketch from nature. She didn't miss her elegant gowns and jewelry, but as time passed she wanted to meet other scientists to exchange information and ideas. She couldn't help wanting to study more insects than she could find in the nearby meadows.

The others in her community believed that nature's beauty was a sign of God's magnificence, but Maria wanted to investigate as well as praise. To grow as a scientist, she needed to talk with others who cared about the things she did. She wanted to see and study a greater variety of plants and animals than could be found in a single place.

After five years, she hugged her friends good-bye and left with her daughters for the bustling port city of Amsterdam. In Holland, she made a living by teaching young ladies how to paint. She met

The boxes of insects intrigued her, but they were dead. Maria wanted to watch them flutter and swoop, and find out what they ate and how they grew and changed.

traders who had brought back not only chocolate, sugar and gold from the New World, but preserved insects and pressed plants, all new and exotic species to the Old World. The boxes of insects intrigued her, but they were dead. Maria wanted to watch them flutter and swoop, and find out what they ate and how they grew and changed. She wanted to see the shapes of the leaves each ate and the vivid colors of their forest homes.

"A woman has no business exploring, or even crossing the Atlantic!" people said. They told stories of pirates and storms with waves as tall as the ship's masts. "You're fifty years old, Maria. Think of your children. Your grandchildren!" But just as Maria had urged her daughters to try new things, now they encouraged her. Dorothea, who was twenty, decided to come with her. Maria sold all her paintings and insect collections. She took out loans and wrote her will.

In 1699, Maria and her daughter set out on a wooden ship. The sky above was wide and blue as it had been when she was young and wondered where the butterflies went. It was time for her to open her own wings instead of struggling to keep them closed. The English and French were settling in North America, but like others from Holland, Maria headed farther south, hoping to see what animals and plants flourished in the hot climate.

After a month on sea, they reached Surinam, a colony in South America. At first, Maria and Dorothea sketched the insects they found on the Dutch sugar plantations. Then they paddled down rivers in dugout canoes. Arawak and Carib guides led them into jungles so thick that they had to hack out paths with axes, looking out for poisonous ants and snakes.

Back at camp, Maria painted insects, iguanas, hummingbirds, lizards, and snails. She happily dipped her brush into dazzling reds and yellows that she had hardly touched before. In each painting she included the leaves or flowers each animal ate to give a sense of the surroundings

She loved the forests, but the extreme heat, which was made worse by her long skirts and full petticoats, was hard on her health. After two years of explorations, Maria became very sick and thought she might die if she stayed longer. She and her daughter returned to Europe with rolled-up paintings, bottles of snakes, and

They entered jungles so thick they had to hack out paths with axes, looking out for poisonous ants and snakes.

boxes filled with preserved butterflies and beetles. Maria made engravings from her sketches for a book called *The Metamorphosis of the Insects of Surinam*. In those days, nature books only showed caterpillars in one section while the butterflies that they became were shown in separate chapters. Maria painted the egg, caterpillar, cocoon, and emerging butterfly together. She showed the insect's whole life on one page, instead of just a part of the metamorphosis.

Maria Sibylla Merian continued to write, paint, and publish work that was admired throughout Europe. She always painted insects along with the plants they needed for food. When she painted flowers, she included the insects they depended upon for pollination. Her understanding of the way life forms changed and the way that those lives were connected to each other helped open a new era in science.

Like a butterfly, Maria kept changing, too: from a girl to wife and mother, artist, scientist, and teacher. She kept an eye on lives so small that few others noticed their beauty. And she kept an eye on the horizon as she wondered what was beyond.

II.

ANNA BOTSFORD COMSTOCK

Among the Six-Legged
(1854-1930)

*L*EAVES FLUTTERED. Branches swayed. Balancing carefully, Anna Botsford looked down at her students. A tree
was an unusual perch for a teacher, but after all, Anna
was just fourteen when she was asked to fill in while the
regular teacher took a few months off.

Anna read books aloud and called out multiplication prob-
lems. When her students finished their sums and spelling, Anna led
them through the woods and fields. She taught them the names of
wildflowers and stars, just as her mother had taught her when she
was small. Anna learned to tell one kind of daisy or bee from
another as naturally as she had learned the names of the man who
ran the mill where the family brought their wheat or the name of
the lady at the general store.

By the time she was seventeen, Anna was teaching full time. A
visitor to her village in upstate New York recognized her intelligence and suggested that she apply to a new university that was
open to women as well as men. Anna was afraid that everyone else
there would have gone to bigger and better schools. She would
miss her parents, and picking apples. She would miss tapping trees
for maple syrup that they boiled in the woods, its fragrance mixed
with the scent of pine trees.

Neighbors said, "What does a farm girl need with college?"
Somehow their comments made Anna more determined. So what
if she had been born in a log cabin? She had read almost every
book in the county, and she wanted to read more. As an only child,

Anna was used to moving straight toward her goals without any-one getting in her way.

But at Cornell University, she was rather shocked to meet girls who shortened their dresses to the tops of their shoes, cut their hair, and argued for women's right to vote. Of course long skirts got in the way as Anna scrambled over rocks or climbed the hilly campus roads. It was a chore to brush and braid her waist-length hair when she would rather be studying mathematics. It wasn't fair that intelligent women could not vote when even the stupid-est man had that right.

But Anna preferred to blend in rather than raise eyebrows. She concentrated on her studies. Her favorite classes were John Henry Comstock's entomology classes, which were often held outdoors, around wasp nests, anthills, and rotten logs. Anna learned that grasshoppers sing with their wings and listen with their knees. Butterflies taste with their feet. Mayflies can't eat during their adult lives. Fleas breathe through holes in their sides and aphids can pro-create without fathers. Anna knew she would never be bored among these animals with six legs and skeletons on the outside. There were millions of species, after all.

She talked with Professor Comstock as they gathered mosses in the gorge and ate together in the dining hall. Before long, the pro-fessor invited Anna to call him Harry, and after several years their friendship turned to love. Instead of going to concerts, they watched fireflies together. And rather than sending Anna roses or chocolates, Harry gave her drawing pens, a drafting board, and a T-square.

Anna found that the act of drawing helped her to look more closely, and to see more. Lovely lines appeared from under her own hands. After they were married, Anna began to illustrate, as well as to help write, Harry Comstock's entomology textbooks. The couple worked as long hours as any farmer, and like farmers, too, they found pleasure in nature. At picnics, they watched yellow jackets perch on dishes to daintily lap fruit juice.

Although they were disappointed not to have children, Anna often set extra plates on the table as their house filled with students and visitors from around the world. Some friends brought fireflies from Cuba, which Anna fastened onto the neckline of her ball

*A tree was an unusual perch for a teacher, but after all, Anna was ju.
few months off.*

urteen when she was asked to fill in while the regular teacher took a

The cucujas seemed to enjoy movement. They glowed most brilliantly when Anna danced.

gown. The cucujas seemed to enjoy movement. They glowed most brilliantly when Anna danced.

After years of doing research with her husband, in 1895 Anna became the first woman to be hired as a professor at Cornell. Unfortunately, some men grumbled that a woman professor would damage the university's reputation—never mind that Anna was one of the most respected and popular teachers. The next year her title and salary were taken back. Naturally, Anna was angry, but just as her father had never complained when things on the farm didn't go right, Anna quietly kept about her teaching and research. She knew that Maria Mitchell taught astronomy at Vassar College. Ellen Swallow taught chemistry and was introducing a study called "Oekologie" at M.I.T. Julia Thomas and Martha Carey Thomas, two of Anna's former suffragist classmates, were now presidents of women's colleges. Even medical schools were finally opening their doors to women. Sooner or later, Anna thought, the Cornell trustees would see that times were changing.

But while Anna was enthusiastic about new opportunities for women, not every change was welcome. As the 1800's ended, many families were leaving farms for jobs in crowded cities. Anna spoke to school teachers who agreed that if their students knew more about nature they might not be so quick to leave the countryside. Most children didn't have mothers like Anna's who encouraged them to wonder about the creatures that live in trees and under fallen leaves. And the trouble was, some teachers confided, they didn't know enough about insects, stars, or rocks to teach much to the children.

So Anna began to write a book, full of questions and answers. "It's good, but it's awfully long," her husband Harry said when the 900 page *The Handbook of Nature Study* was finished. "It will be expensive to print."

Every publisher turned it down. A few said that they might take another look if she cut the manuscript in half. Everyone expected Anna, who still hated to argue, to put the thick manuscript away. But how could she decide which insects to omit when she described only a small portion of the species on our planet? How could she cut chapters about the varieties of trees and birds?

Anna had never dreamed that she would help start a movement to bring nature study into schools.

Anna wouldn't leave the job half-done anymore than her parents would leave apples on the trees. "We'll never sell enough to get back our printing costs," Harry predicted. But he loved Anna, and agreed to help her publish it herself. They moved into a house whose chief attraction was its big, dry basement, perfect for storing books. They began Comstock Publishing with the motto, "Through Books to Nature."

The Comstocks spent their thirty-third wedding anniversary wrapping volumes of *The Handbook of Nature Study*. Thousands of copies quickly sold. When Anna wasn't teaching, she packed cartons and ordered more copies to be printed. Teachers from around the world wrote her warm, thankful letters. In addition, fourteen years after her title of professor was taken away, it was finally given back. Anna's patience and her belief in her own work were rewarded.

Growing up on a small farm, Anna had never dreamed that she would help start a movement to bring nature study into schools. She had never dreamed that in 1920, along with other American women, she would vote for the first time. Three years later, in a poll taken by the League of Women Voters, Anna Botsford Comstock was named as one of twelve greatest living women in the country. She was pleased, but she kept on working the way she always had. Less than two weeks before she died at the age of seventy-six, she was still in a classroom, urging her students to look hard and close at the marvelous world.

III.

FRANCES HAMERSTROM

Secrets
(1907-1998)

FRAN'S LACY DRESS was spotless and smooth. Her back was perfectly straight and her blond hair was tidy. The guests at her mother's tea party asked her questions which she politely answered. Bored, Frances sipped her lemonade until the new maid brought the wrong pitcher from the pantry. Frances watched her pour water into the ladies' crystal glasses. Tadpoles darted among the ice cubes.

Frances hadn't meant to cause trouble when she scooped the baby frogs from the pond, but she often felt like she didn't belong in her family's mansion in Massachusetts. Her mother thought it was proper for her to have a little flowerbed, but when she found her digging in it by herself, she took away her shovel. "Digging holes is the servants' job," her mother said.

Fran's favorite part of gardening was studying the creatures that lived in the soil. Just one shovelful of dirt sometimes turned up beetles, millipedes, and a variety of worms. Fran dug a secret garden behind a shed. Around it, she planted poison ivy, which she was immune to, to discourage visitors.

Keeping secrets became a habit. Fran's mother couldn't understand why, when Fran had a perfectly nice room, she spent hours in treetops. Fran checked on bird nests, collected insects, and used her mother's pearl-handled opera glass to see what the warblers and phoebes were doing. Even Fran's brothers didn't know that she slipped out her window after bedtime and shin-

Tadpoles darted among the ice cubes. Frances hadn't meant to cause trouble.

25

nied down the porch posts. She listened to chirping crickets and cicadas and hooting owls. Sometimes she walked to the marsh, which she called her frog bedroom. She slept under the trees, waking up to see the moon's path as it moved across the sky. She crept back to her room at dawn so that her escape would not be discovered.

By the time Fran was eight, her insect collection filled six shoe boxes. Her pocket-sized insect guide didn't give her the names of all of her specimens, so it was a great day when, after a trip to the dentist in Boston, Fran and her governess stopped at the Natural History Museum. Fran marveled at the rows and rows of insects, labeled with their Latin names. When they got home, she begged her governess to promise that they could come back after her next dentist appointment. Then she locked herself in the bathroom. She jabbed her gums with a pencil. Her mouth hurt, but Fran was overjoyed when her father looked at her red, swollen gums and announced, "You must see the dentist tomorrow."

Fran never completed high school, but she was admitted into Smith College where she flunked out after a year, with 2 A's and 3 F's. She wanted a job so that she could be independent from her parents, but what could she do? She didn't know that there were jobs where people were paid to watch animals, so she used her experience wearing lovely clothes and her ability to walk in high heels without tripping to become a fashion model.

One evening she met Frederick Hamerstrom in a dance hall. Three days later, he proposed marriage. "What took you so long?" Fran teased. She wore a red velvet gown as they waltzed, dreaming of their future. When an opportunity arose for the newlywed couple to study game birds in Wisconsin, Fran packed her elegant red dress along with long winter underwear and sturdy boots. Fran and Frederick moved into a shack with tilting walls and a leaky roof. Basins to catch water were set everywhere, even on their bed. They spent their days looking for prairie chickens to study their habits.

When her mother-in-law wrote advising her to use lace doilies at luncheons, Fran had to laugh. Their kitchen table was covered with axes, hammers, saws, and wildlife magazines. Sometimes they didn't have a dollar to buy a sack of potatoes. Fran lugged a washboard to the lake and rinsed the sheets by running along the shore. Catching her breath, she listened to the loons.

Wisconsin summers were a pleasure, but winters were hard. If Fran spilled a cup of coffee, it froze before she had time to get a mop. One day the water pump froze. It took hours to melt pans of snow into enough water for drinking and washing. Several days passed before a neighbor stopped by. He offered to get their pump going, and asked for kerosene and a rag. Fran brought the kerosene they used for the stove. But having been taught that rags were dirty, Fran had burned all the rags she'd found when they had moved into the old house. She looked through her trunk. She was wearing most of her clothes layered on top of each other. She couldn't give up a sweater or woolen pants. She handed her neighbor the red velvet dress. Without a word, he twisted it around the pump and doused it with kerosene. He lit a match. As the lovely gown burst into flames, Fran thought of how she missed dancing under crystal chandeliers, but she touched Frederick's hand, happy that he loved her in flannel shirts and trousers as much as he had admired her in a fancy gown. Her old loneliness rose with the flames and drifted off with the smoke.

When Fran and Frederick began their studies, most people thought that hunting was the only cause of extinction. Prairie chickens weren't being hunted on the scale that buffalo or whales had been, yet they were quickly disappearing. The Hamerstroms discovered that the clearing of land where the birds traditionally fed and nested had put them in danger. Their studies made it clear that keeping an environment intact is necessary for animals to survive.

Their work began before dawn, and since the birds didn't break for weekends or holidays, neither did they. Fran wasn't slowed down by her pregnancies, and their two children grew up taking for granted that houses were filled with animals. Fran hung fishnets over the office area to keep an owl she had rescued off the typewriter. Once she helped an eagle build her nest. When the family went to the movies, they slipped off their boots and tipped them over to trap mice that came for the spilled popcorn. They brought the mice home to feed to birds of prey.

Their studies made it clear that keeping an environment intact is neces

nimals to survive.

She remembered how, long ago, her mother had told her it was rude to brush your hair in public.

Fran and Frederick Hamerstrom were partners in work and marriage for fifty-nine years. After Frederick died, Fran fulfilled a lifelong dream of seeing a rain forest. She spent a month exploring the Amazon in a dugout canoe.

On a trip to Kenya, she crawled on her hands and knees into her pup tent to brush her hair. She remembered how, long ago, her mother had told her it was rude to brush your hair in public. Fran awkwardly brushed her hair until she thought: I'm ninety years old. I'm in the African jungle. Fran crawled out of the tent and laughed. She stood tall as she brushed her gray hair under the brilliant sky.

IV.

RACHEL CARSON

Signs from the Sea
(1907-1964)

RACHEL CARSON hated the school playground. Nothing grew on gravel or asphalt. And just beyond the teacher's hearing, her classmates teased, "Rachel's legs are so skinny! Where did she find that dress?" Rachel bit her lip and tugged at the dress she knew was a little too big.

Her parents didn't have much money, so most of her clothes were hand-me-downs. Each insult felt like a punch in the stomach. Other girls might fight, shrug, or tease back, but the words that flowed easily at home stuck in Rachel's dry throat when she was on the playground. She counted the minutes until she could go home. Rachel wasn't an only child, like Anna Comstock, but her sister and brother were much older. Rachel was in the habit of being quiet, which helped her to hear the buzz and rustle of small creatures in the trees and grasses of Pennsylvania.

Like Anna Comstock's mother, Rachel's mother had been a teacher who liked to explore the outdoors with her daughter. And when Mrs. Carson couldn't answer Rachel's questions, she referred to Anna Comstock's writing. At night, Rachel and her mother hunted for spiders working on webs or moths that ventured out while birds slept. They listened for the soft sounds of night crawlers dragging leaves through their burrows.

Rachel often hiked past the vegetable garden, lilacs, and roses. She found stones imprinted with sea shells by a river. Rachel had never seen the ocean, but these fossils suggested that the ocean had

At night, Rachel and her mother hunted for spiders working
on webs or moths that ventured out while birds slept.

once covered these Pennsylvania hills. It was comforting to know that time could change things.

Rachel liked the challenge of finding the perfect word for what she saw or thought. When she was ten, she published her first story in "St. Nicholas," a popular children's magazine. Reading and writing continued to be her favorite subjects through high school, and when she began at a nearby women's college, she wrote for the college newspaper and magazine. She enjoyed a science class taught by a professor who encouraged her to change her major from English to biology and to apply for a scholarship at a marine laboratory.

At Woods Hole in Massachusetts, Rachel finally saw the ocean. She waded into a tide pool where thousands of silvery fish, smaller than fingernails, swam around her ankles. Waves rolled in and out. Their sound filled something inside Rachel that she hadn't known was empty. Just as some plants and animals can survive only in particular habitats, maybe some people are supposed to live in certain places, too. Ankle deep in the ocean, Rachel felt at home.

After earning an advanced degree in zoology, Rachel moved to Washington, D.C. She was the first woman, except for the secretaries, hired at a government wildlife agency. At meetings, some men ignored her while others whispered that she must have been hired by mistake, ignoring the fact that she had scored highest on an entry test. Their remarks hurt as much as the teasing in elementary school, but Rachel enjoyed the work itself, especially writing about sea life for radio shows. No one had ever suggested that she could combine her interests in words and nature! Her love of the sea and her vast scientific knowledge spoke to people's hearts and minds.

Her research included putting on an eighty-four pound helmet and diving undersea. In 1949, she was the first woman to travel up the New England coast on the Albatross III, a government research ship. The only problem with her job was that it didn't pay well enough to help her support her recently widowed mother, her sister, and her sister's daughters. To earn more money, Rachel spent most evenings with her cat at her feet, writing books about the sea. She wrote about plants and animals so small that they could only be seen with a microscope, and she wrote about the great forces of

Ankle deep in the ocean, Rachel felt at home.

the water that covers two thirds of the earth. Her second book, *The Sea Around Us*, sold so well that she left her job and moved close to the ocean.

In Maine, she met Dorothy Freeman, who waded with her in tide pools at dawn and watched the stars at night. Dorothy was the first person who seemed to fully understand Rachel's passion for writing and the sea. They talked almost nonstop when they were together, and wrote long letters when they were apart. Alone or with her friend, Rachel explored the Atlantic coast. At first glance there seemed to be no life at all, but a closer look revealed crabs hidden beneath the sand, barnacles clinging to rocks, and protozoa sparkling on the sea's surface. One strand of seaweed might hold thousands of microscopic creatures, as well as periwinkles, starfish, and crabs hiding from sea gulls. Rachel always wondered how each life survived. What did it depend on? Who depended on it? Each question led to other questions as Rachel discovered how all beings need others for food and shelter.

Rachel's quiet, contented life was interrupted in 1957 by a letter from a friend. Many robins had died, her friend said, after the land near her house was sprayed to kill mosquitoes. Rachel stared at this letter the way she had gazed at the fossils she had found when she was young. Then, she had been amazed at how the earth had changed over millions of years. Now, she realized that humans could change the earth in only a few years.

The chemicals that killed the insects also killed birds that ate the insects or drank water that had been contaminated by the sprays. Rachel didn't want to think about the possibility of a world without birds singing, or crickets in the grass, or peepers in the marshes. It was more pleasant to write about the beauty in nature, and people found such writing more enjoyable to read. But how could Rachel enjoy the shores when she knew they were in danger? She had to write, even though her warnings might make some people turn against her. She hoped the book wouldn't take too long.

Five years later, in 1962, *Silent Spring* was published. Rachel showed how pesticides killed useful insects along with harmful ones, leaving the land without bees to pollinate orchards, without spiders and dragonflies to eat mosquitoes. Traces of chemicals left on fruits and vegetables could make people sick.

*She had to write, even though her warnings might make some
people turn against her.*

Because of Rachel's work, new laws to help the environment were passed by the time she died.

As Rachel had predicted, the people who made money selling chemicals were angry. They spent thousands of dollars trying to discredit Rachel by claiming that she was unprofessional, over-emotional, and un-American. Some even said that a woman with no children couldn't possibly care about the future.

These accusations stung like the names Rachel had been called as a schoolgirl. But this time Rachel would not let words stick in her throat. She kept giving speeches. She was often tired and in pain as she fought cancer—an illness she kept secret so that no one could accuse her of being too sick to know what she was talking about. Rachel longed to kick off her high heels and wade by the shore, but she thought of the tiny, silvery fish who made her feel at home when she first saw the ocean. She had to speak for those who couldn't. She had to make sure that every creature always had a home.

Because of Rachel's work, some pesticides were banned. New laws to help the environment were passed by the time she died, two years after *Silent Spring* was published.

Rachel Carson had the courage to change herself and change the world. Her words urge us to look around, to listen closely, and most of all, to wonder. ⭐

V.

MIRIAM ROTHSCHILD

Life in an Old Lawn
(1908-)

By the time the maid finished dusting the many rooms in the Rothschild mansion in England, it was time to start cleaning where she had begun. Dozens of gardeners raked up leaves moments after they touched the ground. They snapped off blossoms the minute they faded.

The Rothschild family was certainly wealthy, but something else was different about them, too. Zebras cantered by the rose bushes. Giant tortoises, brought back from the Galapagos Islands by Miriam's Uncle Walter, lumbered by. Kangaroos leaped through the meadows.

"Does someone really live here?" visitors often asked. There was one greenhouse just for growing green grapes and another for red grapes. One greenhouse was filled with cacti and another was just for growing flowers to send to the Queen on her birthday.

The house itself looked more like a museum or a fairytale palace than a home. It was filled with the sounds of servants' hasty footsteps and the slower footsteps of Miriam's grandmother and uncle. But Miriam's parents were often away, attending to business, waltzing at parties, and adding to their collections.

Miriam often wished she could live in the stables where she thought she would be less lonely. She looked for company under rocks and leaves, and began her first enormous ladybug collection when she was four. Miriam was expected to be as tidy as everything around her, but the grown-ups could hardly complain about either her interest in nature or her desire to collect. Miriam's father

The grown-ups could hardly complain; Miriam's father had collected 30,000 specimens of fleas, after all.

The Rothschild family was certainly wealthy, but something else w[...]

fferent about them, too.

43

had collected 30,000 specimens of fleas, after all. Her Uncle Walter sailed around the world in search of unusual animals and rocks that became part of the biggest donation ever given to the British Museum of Natural History. Miriam was allowed to poke through the thousands of preserved beetles and bird eggs, the millions of butterflies and moths.

Miriam moved to another grand family house when she married. She gave birth to three children and adopted three more. She was as curious about other countries and continents as her father had been, but she wanted to know her children better than her traveling parents had ever known her. Instead of searching for zebras and peacocks, she focused her interests on what she could find right outside her door.

She picked up the cat. She patted the dog. She decided that fleas and other parasites would be her specialty. After getting her six children to bed, she spent the evening peering through a microscope. She often fell asleep right in her chair.

Miriam was the first person to record the extraordinary leaps of fleas. She investigated how they could jump up to ten inches high. That's many, many times the height of a flea: the equivalent of a person vaulting over a skyscraper. Miriam discovered many of the two thousand species of fleas, and she never tired of learning more. After all, she wrote in *Fleas, Flukes, and Cuckoos*, "If we could talk to birds as we talk to each other, we would probably find that fleas ... provide one of the major topics of conversation." Birds eat insects by day, while insects bite birds at night.

As much as she enjoyed researching and writing, the lives of insects did not take all of Miriam's attention. As World War II began, she helped to find safe places for Jewish refugees, including many of her relatives. She worked to change laws so that people fleeing from Nazi Germany could find safety in England. Miriam herself took in forty-nine children. Her big house was temporarily turned into a Red Cross hospital, while some outer buildings housed soldiers. Miriam joined other scientists working to break secret codes. Those were the saddest years of her life.

Many relatives and friends died. Air bases were built on nearby farms, and some of the pilots Miriam met never came back. Finally the war ended, but the terrible times weren't over. Miriam

Through her tears, Miriam watched a caterpillar inch up a buttercup stem, and reached out to a butterfly.

45

worked to get food and clothing to people leaving concentration camps. She wrote letters and organized meetings to find places to live for people whose homes had been destroyed. She was so busy that she hardly had time to go back to her old home until the hospital and military staffs had moved out.

Then, for a few minutes she just stared. Like the whole world, the house and land had changed. The once-immaculate flower beds had been overrun by weeds. Wild grasses covered the tennis court. Walls and statues had been smashed. The windows on the greenhouses were broken, and the house and stables had been ransacked. Miriam felt worse knowing that this destruction had been done by people who were on her side in the war.

She wandered to the pond. The lovely swans had been shot. Miriam sank to the ground right where she stood, among nettles and wild iris, and cried. It seemed that the whole world was coming to an end. All her hope was gone.

Then a speckled butterfly flew over her shoulder. Through her tears, Miriam watched a caterpillar inch up a buttercup stem. She reached out to a butterfly with blue and silver stripes. So life was here, after all. There were no zebras, old tortoises, or elegant swans, but these smaller lives had a beauty all their own. Miriam stood up and walked past looping brambles. She found a wren's nest made entirely of flowers from an oak tree. There was much to marvel at without anyone clipping, pruning, or interfering.

Miriam had the greenhouses repaired, but she left the lawns and tennis courts to wildflowers, weeds, and blue and copper butterflies. She let lilacs, buddleia, wisteria, and ivies climb the stone walls of the house, becoming a home for blackbirds and mice. She studied farming, and realized that it was once common for a hundred kinds of wildflowers to be found in a field where now only hay or clover grew. This not only made the countryside less pretty, but it also ruined the habitat that animals had depended on for centuries. Of course people still grew flowers, but some of the modern varieties tasted so bland that butterflies wouldn't bother with them and left the area.

Miriam discovered that many species of butterflies were dying out. She and some helpers collected seeds from abandoned World War II airfields. Using these, Miriam grew 120 species of wild-

Miriam would be up at dawn, watching the starlings that roosted by the thousands in the trees around her house.

flowers on what she calls her "ex-lawns." Each year these seeds are collected by hand, packaged, and sold. Her goal isn't to make a profit selling seeds, but every time people plant flowers loved by butterflies, the butterflies have a better chance of living.

Some neighbors tease Miriam about what they call her weed farm, but through her writing and public speaking, Miriam has raised awareness of the need for butterfly gardens and wildflower meadows. In addition to this work, Miriam wrote many books about a wide variety of subjects. She's devoted herself to political work such as improving conditions for the mentally ill and helping to make laws against discrimination towards lesbians and gay men. Her oldest daughter inspired her to become a vegetarian, and Miriam lectures to promote better treatment of animals in laboratories and on farms.

Years ago she designed a simple, comfortable dress and jacket, and had several made in different fabrics. She wears one of these dresses every day so that she won't have to waste a minute deciding what to wear. She sleeps only four or five hours a night, then is up at dawn, reading, or watching the starlings that roost by the thousands in the trees around her house. There is always more to know, always more to discover.

Sometimes visitors drive up the bumpy road. They stare at the tangle of weeds and ivy that seem to have overtaken the house and garden. "Surely no one can live here?" people often say. Someone certainly does, among the butterflies and birds: a brilliant woman who sometimes wonders what will happen to the wildflowers after she dies. Will the daisies and bluebells be mown down? Or will someone plant new flowers? One thing is certain: change is bound to come. A garden has a life of its own.

VI.

JANE GOODALL

The Dream
(1934-)

ANE GOODALL loved to watch spiders scramble, beetles scatter, and worms slither. At age five, she was used to hearing her mother call, "Jane! Where are you?" But the panic in her mother's eyes when she found her one day was unusual. "I was in the hen house," Jane said. She liked to sift through the straw for the warm, smooth eggs, then carry them home as carefully as if she held treasures. But that afternoon she hadn't been collecting eggs.

"I was about to call the police!" her mother said. "What on earth were you doing?"

"I wanted to see the hen lay an egg," Jane confessed.

"But you were gone all afternoon!"

Jane nodded. She knew chickens rushed off if followed, so she had hidden hours before and sat so quietly that she hadn't been spotted.

"And you saw a hen lay an egg?" When Jane smiled, her mother smiled, too. She didn't scold Jane for making her worry. Instead, she pulled her close and said, "Tell me about it."

With a knack for quiet, concentrated observation—and an understanding mother—five-year-old Jane was well on her way to a career as a naturalist. Her grandmother was a careful watcher, too. When she noticed how often Jane climbed a beech tree in her yard, she gave her the tree as her own. And seeing that Jane had checked a Doctor Doolittle book out of the library several times, her grandmother gave her the book for Christmas. Jane liked to wander

*She had hidden hours before and sat so quietly that she hadn't
been spotted.*

through the meadows pretending that she, too, could talk to African animals. She carefully watched insects and squirrels, while dreaming that someday she, like Tarzan, would hear nothing but wind in the trees and animals calling to each other. Jane started a nature club with her younger sister and two friends. She named it the Alligator Club, even though she knew she wouldn't find alligators in England! The four girls started a magazine which included nature notes, sketches of insects, and quizzes. They set up a museum.

Jane made her little sister ask passersby to visit, then collected a donation to a society that protected old horses. The visitors admired the pressed flowers and bird eggs, held seashells to their ears, and petted the guinea pigs. The most famous exhibit was a human skeleton donated by Jane's uncle who had studied to be a doctor.

Jane did well enough in school, though her mother had to call her many times before she got out of bed (unlike on weekends, when Jane was up early to head outdoors). After graduating from high school, she trained as a secretary. She held jobs typing letters for doctors, filing papers at a university, then editing documentaries at a London film studio. When she was twenty-three, a friend invited her to visit her family's new farm in Kenya. Jane moved back home to save money, took a job as a waitress, learned to balance a dozen plates of food at once, and saved her tips. In 1957, she headed off to Africa.

In Kenya, she arranged to visit Louis Leakey, a scientist well-known for his work studying the origin of humans. His secretary had left the day before, so he hired Jane. Soon, in addition to typing, Jane rescued hurt animals. Once she collected crickets for an orphaned galago, or bush baby. She forgot that the crickets were in her purse when she went on a date. When the crickets escaped, Jane scrambled under the table to collect them.

There was no second date, but Louis Leakey was impressed by Jane's love for animals. He invited her to join him and his wife, the anthropologist Mary Leakey, on an expedition to dig fossils. Jane loved the long hours of hard work outdoors. Louis Leakey told her of his hope to understand more about early humans by studying primates such as chimpanzees, gorillas, and orangutans. He raised money so that Jane could spend six months in the forest.

It seemed like a dream come true, but officials in Tanzania said that it wasn't safe for a woman to work alone there. Worried, Jane confided the problem in a letter to her mother. A few weeks later, Jane and her mother were packing old army tents, green and brown clothes, binoculars, and stacks of notebooks into a Land Rover. They set off with a guide and cook for Gombe National Park where Jane spent her days wandering. After a few weeks, the guide grew bored and stayed at the campsite, to Jane's relief. It was easier to be as quiet as the trees around her when she was alone.

On days when she didn't see an animal, Jane was glad that she could confide her disappointments to her mother when she returned to camp. And when she crept a little closer to a monkey, mongoose, or chimpanzee, it was exciting to tell her all about it.

Her mother set up a clinic where she handed out aspirin and bandages. The native people got to know the caring older woman, then gradually accepted the daughter who spent her days rather uselessly, it seemed to them, scrambling through the hills with only binoculars, a water bottle, a pencil and a notebook.

After many weeks of walking and waiting, a few chimpanzees began to view Jane as part of the forest. "Talking to animals" was mostly a matter of listening and watching closely. Each step closer to the chimpanzees made every long, lonely day worthwhile. She watched a chimpanzee using sticks to dig out termites, and telegrammed the news to Louis Leakey. Until that moment, scientists had believed that humans were the only animals to use tools.

Jane's discovery helped her to get money to stay longer. It was clear now that six months wouldn't be enough time to get to know the chimpanzees. Jane sadly said good-bye when her mother returned to England, but she rarely felt lonely among the trees. She was thrilled by each act of trust from a chimpanzee, from a hand reaching for a banana to a mother cautiously letting Jane briefly hold her baby.

As the years passed, Jane realized that there was more to do than one person could do alone. Several other researchers set up tents near hers. They took notes on what they saw while Jane made some trips back to England, where she was working toward a degree so that scientists would take her discoveries more seriously. She enjoyed seeing family and old friends, and was relieved to see that she remembered to look both ways before crossing streets and didn't toss apple cores onto carpets. But she was happiest when she got back to the chimpanzees who had become like friends to her.

Jane was reluctant to give up her solitude when the National Geographic Society asked to send a photographer.

She was reluctant to give up more solitude when people from the National Geographic Society asked to send a photographer. She agreed only because she wanted people to see the tenderness and intelligence that chimpanzees showed in their natural environment. Jane was pleased to find that Hugo Van Lawick cared as much about animals as she did. As Hugo watched the chimps with Jane, taking pictures and movies, the two fell in love. They got married in England, celebrating with a traditional wedding cake, but with a statue of a chimpanzee on top. Three days later, they were both happy to get back to work in Africa.

The next year, Jane gave birth to a baby they called Grub. She and Hugo raised their baby partly inspired by the devotion that chimpanzee mothers showed their young. As Grub grew up, the family moved from tents into a cabin. Jane's husband often traveled to photograph animals all across Africa. Finding it hard to spend time together, he and Jane divorced when Grub was seven.

A few years later, Grub went to live with Jane's mother in England to attend school. The research center at Gombe National Park continued to expand. In 1986, Jane realized that she had lived her dream of sharing life with African animals for twenty-five years. The chimpanzees she had known at Gombe would be safe, since the park was protected. But many forests around it were being cut down. The chimpanzees could not survive without homes.

Just as Rachel Carson gave up her quiet life beside the ocean to spend years working on *Silent Spring*, Jane Goodall left the forest and animals she loved in order to help save them. Today she spends most days living out of suitcases. She takes planes between Africa, Europe, and North America to speak for animals who know kindness and fear but not words. She tells people about the range of feelings chimpanzees show in their natural surroundings, and she protests the limited freedom some have in circuses, zoos, and research laboratories.

In addition to lecturing, Jane writes about her life and what she's learned about and from the chimpanzees. Like the patient and passionate naturalists before her, Jane Goodall believes that if people can see the beauty that she sees, they will work to save the animals and trees that give them food and shelter. She shows how one woman's hope can spread around the world.

Many forests around the park were being cut down. The chimpanz

...uld not survive without homes.

A Note from the Author

The people in this book are real and all events actually happened. In some cases I used fictional techniques, such as writing dialogue, to highlight discoveries and accomplishments.

Here is a list of sources I consulted and where you can learn more about these women naturalists. —JA

Recommended Reading

Maria Sibylla Merian
Maria Sibylla Merian's artwork can be viewed in museums around the world, including the National Museum of Women in the Arts in Washington, D.C. This museum offers a Web site at www.nmwa.org, where you can find a short biography of Maria Sibylla Merian and see some of the plants and insects she painted.

More information can be found in books that feature women artists, such as *Women Artists* by Karen Petersen and J. J. Wilson (New York: Harper and Row, 1976).

The fullest account of Maria Sibylla Merian's life is in *Women on the Margins: Three Seventeenth Century Lives* by Natalie Zemon Davis (Cambridge, Mass.: Harvard University Press, 1995).

Anna Botsford Comstock
An account of Anna Botsford Comstock's life is in *Women in the Field: America's Pioneering Women Naturalists* by Marcia Myers Bonta (College Station, Texas: Texas A&M University Press, 1992).

Comstock, Anna Botsford *The Comstocks of Cornell: John Henry Comstock and Anna Botsford Comstock* (Ithaca, N.Y.: Comstock Publishing Associates, 1953).

Frances Hamerstrom

Hamerstrom, Frances *My Double Life: Memoirs of a Naturalist* (Madison, Wisconsin: The University of Wisconsin Press, 1994).

Hamerstrom, Frances *Walk When the Moon is Full* (New York: Crossing Press, 1976).

Rachel Carson

Good books include *Rachel Carson: Pioneer of Ecology* by Kathleen Kudlinski (New York: Puffin Books, 1997), which is written for young people, and biographies for adults such as *Rachel Carson: Witness for Nature* by Linda Lear (New York: Henry Holt and Co., 1997)

All of Rachel Carson's books are readily available. Her last book, *The Sense of Wonder* (New York: HarperCollins, 1998) is the shortest, but it powerfully shows what Rachel Carson valued.

Miriam Rothschild

Essays about Miriam Rothschild can be found in *Brave Companions: Portraits in History* by David McCullough (New York: Simon and Schuster, 1992) and *Ornament and Silence: Essays on Women's Lives* by Kennedy Fraser (New York: Alfred A. Knopf, 1997).

Some of Rothschild's essays about the lives of butterflies are included in *Butterfly Gardening: Creating Summer Magic in Your Garden* (ed. Xerces Society, San Francisco, Calif.: Sierra Club Books, 1998).

Jane Goodall

Jane Goodall's wonderful books include *My Life with the Chimpanzees* (New York: Pocket Books, 1996) and *The Chimpanzee Family Book*, with photographs by Michael Neugebauer (New York: North South Books, 1997).

You can find out more about her work and how to help at her web site at www.janegoodall.org.

Of course there are more women naturalists than the six profiled here! Look for these books to learn more about other women who care for the earth.

Breton, Mary Joy *Women Pioneers for the Environment* (Boston: Northeastern University Press, 1998).

Keene, Ann T. *Earthkeepers: Observers and Protectors of Nature* (New York: Oxford University Press, 1994).

Sirch, Willow Ann *Eco-Women: Protectors of the Earth* (Golden, Colorado: Fulcrum Publishing, 1996).

About the Author

Jeannine Atkins was a girl who looked under rocks. Particular trees and stones outside her house were as familiar as her bedroom and made good spots to wonder. When she grew up, writing became her way to keep exploring and dreaming. She particularly likes combing libraries for stories about amazing girls and women. In addition to this book, they have inspired her picture books which include *Aani and the Tree Huggers* and *Mary Anning and the Sea Dragon*. She lives with her husband and their daughter in Massachusetts.

About the Illustrator

Paula Conner's parents are gifted professional musicians, so her love for music and songwriting seemed natural. It was a delightful surprise as a young adult, however, to discover that she could draw. With no formal training, she has been a commissioned portrait artist for more than twenty-five years, although this is her first published work as an illustrator. Her medium of choice is charcoal because it allows her to capture light and shadow dramatically, bringing a three-dimensional, lifelike quality to her work. To capture a poignant expression, a fleeting display of emotion in the eyes, is what excites her. A mother of four and a devoted wife, her greatest love will always be her family; but her art is unquestionably another.

Other Distinctive Nature Awareness Books

John Muir: My Life with Nature, by Joseph Cornell. This unique "autobiography" of John Muir is told in his own words, brimming with his spirit. Compiled by naturalist Joseph Cornell, this book captures an aliveness, a presence of goodness, adventure, enthusiasm, and sensitive love of each animal and plant that will give young adults an experience of a true hero unlike any found today.

Sharing Nature with Children and Sharing Nature with Children II, by Joseph Cornell. This is the classic parents' and teachers' nature awareness guidebook, now in its second (20th Anniversary) edition, and its sequel, filled with nature games.

Play Lightly on the Earth, by Jacqueline Horsfall, endorsed by Joseph Cornell, is written especially with 3 to 9 year olds in mind, and based on sound scientific concepts with an emphasis on creative thinking, problem-solving, and skill development—all in the guise of play.

My Monarch Journal, by Connie Muther, shows in stunning photography the metamorphosis of a caterpillar becoming a butterfly—one of nature's most dramatic miracles. It is a write-in journal for students following the development of their own monarch, with easy instructions for parents and teachers. Available in both student (32 p.) and parent-teacher (52 p.) editions.

Stickeen, John Muir and the Brave Little Dog, by John Muir as retold by Donnell Rubay. Stranded on a glacier, John Muir and a little dog handle the challenge and are changed by it. This classic true story, now with superb

om Dawn Publications

illustrations, was "the most memorable of all my wild days," Muir later wrote.

A Walk in the Rainforest, A Swim through the Sea, and *A Fly in the Sky*—the popular trilogy of habitat books written and illustrated by the young author, Kristin Joy Pratt. Each book presents its habitat in alphabetical and alliterative format. (Teacher's Guides available for each book.)

A Tree in the Ancient Forest, by Carol Reed-Jones, uses repetitive, cumulative verse to show graphically the remarkable web of interdependent plants and animals that all call a big old tree home.

Places of Power, by Michael DeMunn, reveals the places of power that native people all over the world have always known exist, and explores with children how to become attuned to this place of power.

My Favorite Tree, by Diane Iverson. The native trees of North America have given us food, shelter and an important part of our heritage. Naturalist-illustrator Diane Iverson's book is both useful and fun, combining a sweet intimacy with interesting facts about 27 major trees and their relatives.

Dawn Publications is dedicated to inspiring in children a deeper understanding and appreciation for all life on Earth. To order, or for a copy of our catalog, please call 800-545-7475, or visit our web site at www.dawnpub.com.